Ghost Frequencies

Justin LeDuc

BookLeaf Publishing

India | USA | UK

Presentation by *BookLeaf Publishing*

Web: www.bookleafpub.com

E-mail: info@bookleafpub.com

ISBN: 9789357447157

First edition 2022

DEDICATION

In Loving Memory of

Garry LeDuc Sr.

PREFACE

Just as the pandemic was starting to effect my life I was given a solely solitary problem of my own when I was diagnosed with Stage 4 cancer. The following poems are a compilation of the thoughts and emotions that permeated throughout my treatment, recovery, and eventual return to society. Mental health, the flaws of the world around me, and a newly shifted focus and perspective all contributed to these existential and ideological utterances of mind that I hope will inspire others to let go of the need for success and take solace in the act of expression itself as the reward.

I Am Tired

The stirring pain and throbbing beat,
The pillow drenched beneath my head,
I sit up with the same chorus rambling through
my mind as the night before,
I am tired.
Each breath stirs the shallow pit above my heart
that sends the skin to tremors.
I am tired.
I try to steer my mind away
From all the randomness that decays the focus.
Unchecked, each tingle and tinge thrashes me,
caught in this anxious gator's maw.
I am tired.
As I numb myself to ease the noise
I fear one day the weight of my chest will crush
me.
And just as my mind swells, the jitters evolve
into a quiver, into a quake, and the day comes to
a close.
In my bed I lie awake,
Eyes are closed hoping for rest, when the abyss
of thought reminds me that tomorrow,
I will be tired.

Writer's Tears

The lenten bask in their moment of reprieve. A
day where culture and happiness outway faith
and devotion
As a sea of green reaches out in revelry.

I choke a subtle sigh.
A cold brisk éire, and I'm spinning again
Into the twisting serpentine fears of diasporic
displacement.

The days since last year have gathered dust on
my bones.
I hear the penny whistle eternally
As I sweep the year's shadows away in the flow
of my Writer's Tears

Ghost Frequencies

True serenity
Undisturbed by whispered steps
With a primal significance
Intently traversing through my
Dimensional distortion
Walk through space as though you were never
there
And find yourself hidden in the air
Find my ghost frequency
A space all my own
Shifted out of view, displacing real
Sequestered beyond perception
Walk through life as though you were never
there
And let them find you hidden in the air
Deliberate
Unobstructed existence in mind

Ants Burn

Amidst a dull and listless atmosphere, grey
Saturated misery unrelenting
Kill the pain, Unhinge your brain
Find the wire
Confidant enough to fall
Wholly into true objectivity
To stop the ring
From crushing me
Selfless psychosis fever, fuming surrounded
Ignarrogance defined, neologist
Sputum of mindless obtusion
Free me from this dense confusion
Give me the pain needed to rise above fools
Before they start crushing me
Each tear gives me the foresight
Sense to say fuck it to the hindsight
Every nightmare I survive just makes me
brighter
See them hold the script upside down, try to help
them turn around
They revert to infantile, empty worded
arguments
The once enraged now amused by enforced
accountability
Shining justified superiority upon the ground

Laughing as the ants burn

Fear the Mindkiller

Scored in history
Our missteps seeding regrets
To which we etch our philosophies and lessons
Fear of our past feeds the tree
Of time our mind inhabits, locked isolated
Between memories
Breeding doubt and decay in our thoughts
distracted
From dreams so simple
Forever in the future

Scrapes and Bruises

My face tenses against the petrified creak
As stiffened aches and brittle joints
Crackle and twist rigidly
The scrapes and bruises only fuel my refractory
outlook
As the sag in my eyes deepens
My grin drifts carelessly firm
The pain of staying numb to the immalleable is
exhausting enough

New Built Sigh

The air
Cool and comforting as the whistling birds
Fill a cascading tone
Chuckled and grinned
I hold tight the air in hope of depths
Unimaginable in objective joy
The ground
Softer and welcoming to my slowing steps
Seized in a fragile calm
Buckled and bruised
I brace hard against the fiendish thoughts
Threatening my new built sigh
The grin is my new champion, angered
expectation the fist
Still learning to pull punches

Caring for the Careless

A burning blind epiphany
Agelessly evoking diversion
Indulgently free
Bold compassion exuding
Embracing our cherished
Deeply devoted
Feral and enraged
Tooth-barred to the disputants
Firm in hand
To feel is human, denial malignant
Why waste your energy caring for the careless
who would disregard you in return?

Wrinkles

The sun warms those moments
Making the wrinkles in your breath and aches in
your limbs summon a humble grin
Basking cool in the evening sky
Each tender throb and I face my weakness
Emboldened impervious in my own slow decay
Our mortality only makes us more immortal

Yours is the Voice I Hear

Yours is the voice I hear
The duality within the inner monologue
Adrift amidst the endless debate
Worry and confidence, regret and pride
The many inflections of my own tongue
thrashing my mind
Overlaying a subtle yet distinct vibration
Fiery in its determination and drive resonating
behind the conscious
Yours is the voice I hear
When my voice of reason is filled with doubt
Stone-hearted in tear-shredded skin
My voice of resolve and rebellion boosts bold in
its slap of sense
Except radiating deep inside that sense of life
Yours is the voice I hear

Sun-Licked and Sore

Sun-licked and sore
Staring into the grinning moon
Cool night air caressing the radiant heat seething
from my pores
Embracing my twilit boon
Casting off from my tangled shores
Weightlessly gilded under anxious clouds and
familiar tunes
Sigh away the dissonance and find instant
gratification

Teacher of Self

Naturally inclined instinctual
Inquisitive in foot
Eyes wide with light and love
Guide of my own resolve
My teacher of self
With lessons of how to answer
All my own questions
Knowledge granted in wealth
Mother, shipwright amidst
Perilous shores of potential
Steered compassionately with a strength
Whose memory is now essential
Remind yourself, In vehement defiance
Trust your ship to bring you home

Amidst the Chill

Gradual echo extends
Extruding apprehension
Dispersed in clouds of restless rain
Deflated, momentum dissipates
Mind settles joyfully idle
Eyes gazing toward neglected horizons
Grazing carefree amidst the chill

時

Flickering golden
Times flame waverless to will
Fluid form indefined
Fools grasp with burned hands
Lost chasing static mirage
Time wasted for all
Temporal waves flow
Drift careless the muddied banks
Searing light of joy

Fresh Eyes

Dreams calling with sleeps sweet song
Serene and gratifying
Too easy the wish trickles
An endless drift in unconsciousness
The idyll a facade
It's existence reliant on the conscious slumber
Dreaming refuses awakening
To seek it demanding blindness
Dissolve the island of your yearning
With fresh eyes face the sea
The future rests in your reflection
Not in your eye lids

The Ring

The ringing finally softens
In the nothing.
The void grounds the buzz
And slows chimes with each
Exhale.

Flicker and blur
Expand and weaze through buttered lungs
In reflection I gaze joyfully calmed

Sabbatical

Tensions high, patience bent
Like the ear the devil on my shoulder rents
Whispering the motivation needed to drift in and
out of conscious existence.

Stance firm and tolerance low
The devil's neighbor shrugs in defeat
Compassion and altruism with none deserving,
the angel sigh in my other ear.

Existential sabbatical
Whimsically aloft with nymphs of morality
Balanced atop a selfish fulcrum, devoid of guilt
and responsibilities.

Step back through with ambiguity and apathy
The angel and devil now stand guard
Diligent in defense of what little energy remains

Home - A Haiku

Recede from the light
Peripheral from judgment
The welcomed abyss